Vintage Cards
to Make and Treasure

Judy Balchin, Barbara Gray,
Paula Pascual, Joanna Sheen
and Patricia Wing

Contents

Materials

At the beginning of each project is a 'you will need' list so that you know what to gather together before making your vintage card. Below are some general guidelines for cardmaking materials, and on the following pages there is more specific advice on what you need for the cards in each section of the book. Remember that cardmaking is all about creativity, and if exact replicas of the materials shown are not available, you can always choose similar alternatives.

Basic materials

You will need some basic cardmaking materials such as a craft knife and cutting mat and a metal ruler for measuring and cutting card and paper. Some authors like to use a guillotine. You will need ordinary scissors and some projects specify other types such as decollage craft scissors, embroidery scissors, decoupage snips or fine scissors. Some cards require a circle cutting system. Other general materials are a graphite pencil, retractable pencil, watercolour pencils, coloured pencils, a gold leafing pen, acrylic paints and a paintbrush, chalk with a small foam eye-shadow applicator, a make-up sponge, a $\frac{1}{16}$in hole punch, a Japanese screw punch or eyelet punch and hammer, tweezers, a bone folder, an eraser and a water brush.

Paper and card

A wide variety of cards and papers are required for vintage cardmaking, which is half the fun! For the projects in this book, cardmakers have used A4 and A5 sheets of 300gsm (140lb) cold-pressed watercolour paper, brown card, black card, gold metallic card, gold mirror card, dark brown card, orange textured card, lilac card, pale blue glitter card, rainbow card, white card, maroon card, green card, silver card, dark blue card, dark green card, pink pastel card, white pearl card, pale coral card, red pearly card, antique gold card, duck-egg blue card and off-white card. You will also need scrap paper, greaseproof paper, lilac textured paper, lace paper, pink lace paper, purple marbled paper, lined pink lace paper, green handmade paper, copper metallic paper, William Morris design backing paper, transparency paper, photocopier paper and lilac parchment. Some projects specify ready-made card blanks, and those shown are light green, burgundy, pearlescent dark green and cream. When collecting together your cards and papers, you will need to find sheets of acetate for some of the cards.

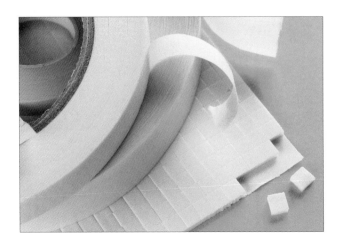

Adhesives

These are very important for cardmaking, and most crafters have their favourites for different purposes. Some of the adhesives used in the vintage cards in this book are: double-sided sticky tape, low-tack masking tape, low tack tape, sticky foam pads, sticky foam tape, silicone glue, spray glue, crafter's glue, strong, clear glue, PVA glue with a fine-tip applicator, a cocktail stick, large glue dots, an adhesive roller, a pinpoint roller glue pen and an ordinary glue pen.

Rubber stamping equipment

The authors of this book list the specific stamps and inkpads they have used in their projects, but you can of course choose similar alternatives. In the Clear Stamped Cards section, for the Fashion project you will need: the tailor's dummy and ornate corner clear stamps, a dye-based sepia archival inkpad and a dye-based currant inkpad; for the Mail Art card: large and small postage stamp and la petite musique clear stamps, a dye-based plum inkpad and dye-based cabin fever rainbow inkpad; for the Victorian Lace card: rose, topaze and Victorian corner clear stamps and a dye-based eggplant inkpad. In the Fairy Cards section, for the Forest Fairy card, you will need: Fairy rubber stamp: Personal Impressions P735G, a scroll pattern rubber stamp: Penny Black 2636K, a black inkpad, embossing pad and gold embossing powder. In the Celtic Cards section, for the Emerald Cross card you will need a Celtic cross rubber stamp, e.g. Heritage Rubber Stamp Co., Celt5XLS1 and a circular Celtic spiral rubber stamp, e.g. Heritage Rubber Stamp Co., Celt3XLS4; for the Copper Script card you will need a large background script rubber stamp, e.g. Heritage Rubber Stamp Co., Celt6XLS1. In the Cards for All Occasions section, for the Moving Day card, you need an acrylic mounting block and country cottage themed stamps. Other more general rubber stamping and heat embossing equipment includes: a watermark inkpad, an archival royal blue inkpad, dusty pink embossing powder, dark green and light green embossing powders, a heat tool/gun, a brayer and large sticky yellow notes.

Embellishments

Cards can be decorated with all kinds of embellishments. The vintage cards in this book feature: brads, silver star gems and sequins, iridescent sequins, small green sequin stars, small adhesive craft jewels and self-adhesive pearls; small gold beads, pearl beads, pearl seed beads, lilac seed beads, lilac beads and a needle and thread for sewing on beads; lilac organza ribbon, pale blue organza ribbon, burgundy ribbon, gold ribbon, paper lace ribbons, bronze ribbon and pale blue ribbon; narrow ruffled lace and a piece of white lace; snowy glitter and fine white glitter; small pieces of imitation gold leaf, sheets of white shrink plastic, a small white doily, a key embellishment, buttons, gold wire, cord and gold photo corner craft stickers.

Special materials

As well as the general materials that are common to most cardmaking, there are some specific materials recommended in this book. Remember that, even with materials such as stamps, templates and images, you can choose alternatives if you cannot find the exact replicas.

Celtic Cards

The Silver Gate card uses a circular Celtic brass stencil, e.g. Dreamweaver, LL380 and a rectangular Celtic brass stencil, e.g. Marianne Designs, CT6004. For the Emerald Cross project, you will need green pearlescent pigment powder and gum arabic (fixative) mixed to make pearlescent watercolour paint. For the Copper Script card, you will need Circular Celtic brass stencil, e.g. Dreamweaver, LL520 with lightweight copper sheet, large and fine stump tools and round-ended and pointed embossing tools. You will also need alcohol inks in four different shades (reds, browns and oranges), an alcohol ink applicator, blending solution and a cotton bud. Finally you require silver and black embossing paste, a spatula, a palette knife, an embossing tool and a foam mat.

Beaded Cards

This section requires paper piercing and some embossing equipment. For the Cameo Card the author has used pricking templates PR0507 and PR0509 and a pricking tool and mat. You will also need a pink cameo. For the Lilac and Lace card, you will need stencils that are for both pricking and embossing, 5802S and EF8013, to be used with a light box and embossing tool, and also pricking template PR0507. In all cases, alternatives in a similar shape and size are quite acceptable.

Victorian and Fairy Cards and Cards for all Occasions

In the Victorian Cards section of the book, Joanna Sheen uses designs that were printed out from a Victorian-themed CD of images, but you can also search the internet, where many vintage images are available to buy or even to download for free. You can search antique shops or junk shops. For the Fancy Photograph card, you will need the flower frame and printed photograph of a girl; for the Baby Lace card, you will need two baby images; and for the Decoupage Kitten card, you will need kitten images especially for decoupage. Judy Balchin's Snow Fairy project in the Fairy Cards section of the book uses images from a CD, but there are also many vintage fairy images available online. For the Moving Day card in the Cards for all Occasions section, you need one sheet of country cottage-themed decoupage, including a sheet of backing paper. For the Christmas Card, you will need one 30 x 21cm (12 x 8¼in) church scene picture, for the Happy Anniversary card, you will need three identical Victorian-style photographs of a courting couple, and suitable vintage photographs will also be needed for the Congratulations card.

CLEAR STAMPED CARDS

by Barbara Gray

The art of stamping is, I am told, the most popular and fastest-growing pastime in the world of crafting. During the past twenty years, it has evolved into a sophisticated art form, and using clear stamps opens up countless creative doors, because you can see right through to the surface you are stamping on to align the images perfectly.

Over the years that I have been designing clear stamps, I have developed many ways to use them, and this section will feature some of my tips and techniques which can only be performed with clear stamps.

You can spend a mint on accessories and supplies for your vintage cards (if you haven't already!), but all you really need is a stamp, an inkpad, some paper and a quiet half-hour to start. When you first begin, I recommend that you just try playing with your stamp. Try not to judge your first work against the projects shown here: I spent many hours on them, and that was after fifteen years of practice! Just relax and enjoy the art. Skill comes with experience, but fun can be had along the way.

I hope that these vintage themed projects motivate you to try making your own works of art, and when you have·mastered the techniques in this section, why not borrow one of my recipes and add some spice of your own?

Remember, it is about the journey, not the destination. Good luck!

Fashion

In this chapter, I want to show you how to completely alter a stamp by filling the image with another stamp – another technique that is only possible with a transparent stamp.

An ornate corner stamp is used again in this chapter to emphasise their flexibility.

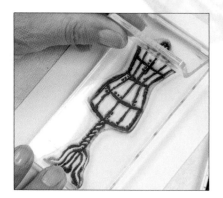

1 Use the tailor's dummy stamp with the sepia ink and stamp right in the centre of the 15 x 10cm (6 x 4in) piece of watercolour paper.

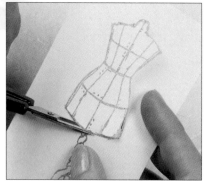

2 Stamp it again on a large sticky note and use a pair of embroidery scissors to cut out the body (not the stand) of the dummy to make a mask.

YOU WILL NEED

Clear stamps: tailor's dummy, ornate corner

A4 sheets of 300gsm (140lb) cold-pressed watercolour paper

A4 brown card

Dye-based sepia archival inkpad

Dye-based currant inkpad

Make-up sponge

Gold leafing pen

Three brads

Embroidery scissors

Paintbrush

Large sticky yellow notes

Double-sided sticky tape

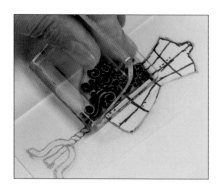

3 Position the mask over the impression on the watercolour paper and place other sticky notes over the rest of the paper to protect it. Ink the ornate corner stamp with sepia ink, blot it, then position the tip in the centre of the dummy's waist as shown to stamp the bottom left part of the dummy.

4 Ink and blot the stamp again, then turn the stamp through ninety degrees and stamp the tip in the centre to mark the bottom right part of the dummy.

5 Stamp the top corners in the same way to complete the pattern.

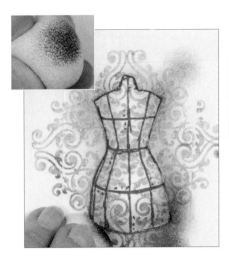

6 Pinch the corners of the make-up sponge in your fingers to force the centre out into a mushroom shape (see inset). Dab this into the currant ink, blot it on scrap paper and dab it gently round the edges of the tailor's dummy.

Tip
Build the colour up gradually with the sponge. You can add colour, but you can not take it away.

7 Peel off all of the sticky notes, then cover the dummy in the centre with a new note (see inset). Place the card on scrap paper and use the ornate corner stamp with sepia archival ink to stamp each of the corners and the two long edges. Remember to blot the stamp.

8 Ink blot and stamp the space between impressions, looking through the stamp to make sure that the pattern matches up well with the existing stamped impressions (see inset).

9 Use the make-up sponge with currant ink to gradually build up colour around the inside border.

10 Remove the large sticky note and use a damp paintbrush to pick up a little currant ink and paint the stand.

11 Push the nib of the gold leafing pen down on the side of the card and drag it all the way round to edge the card.

12 Use the point of your embroidery scissors to pierce the dummy where the seams cross the centre of the chest.

13 Push a brad through the hole and secure.

14 Repeat twice more to complete the artwork, then make a brown card and attach the artwork with double-sided sticky tape to finish the card.

Kasha and the Leafy Corner

*This entire card was created using just two stamps
(the lady and the leafy corner) and different parts of
a rainbow inkpad. Oh – and hours of focus and fun!*

The Geisha in Love

The Geisha's dress is painted in folds, and only the folds are filled with the love symbol.

Paris in the Spring

The Parisian lady's dress is filled using the same honeysuckle stamp used on the notelets on pages 28–29.

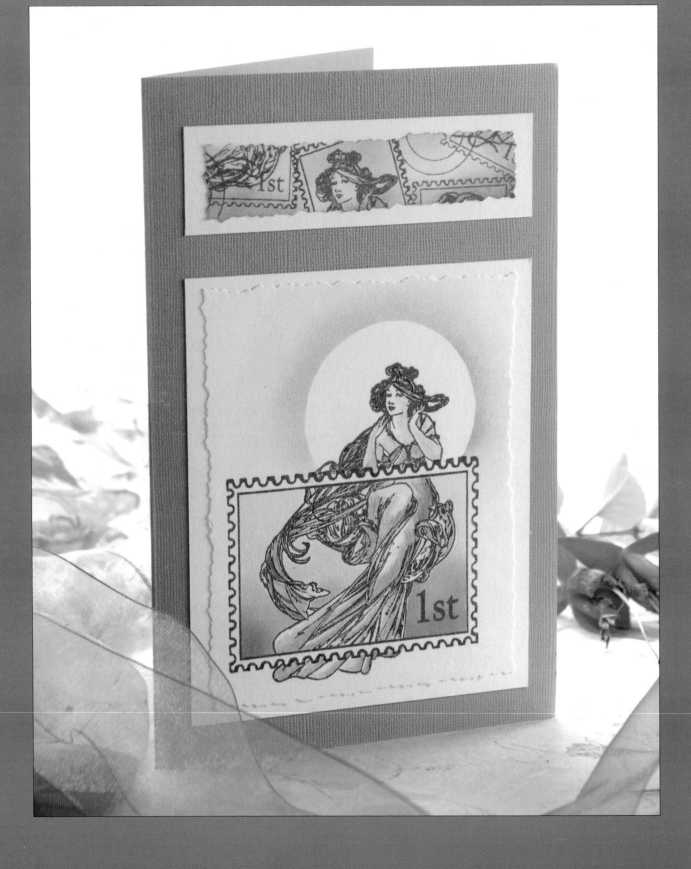

Mail Art

I always have great fun creating faux postage stamps, and it is even more creative when you can stray beyond the box with a clear stamp as I have done here.

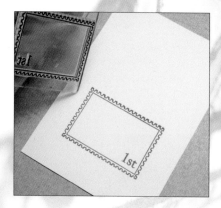

1 Cut your watercolour paper in half to get an A5 sheet, and stamp a large postage stamp towards the bottom with sepia ink.

2 Stamp a second identical postage stamp on scrap paper and use scissors to cut out the centre to make a large mask.

3 Use masking tape on the back to secure the mask in place over the watercolour paper. Use sepia ink with the la petite musique stamp to stamp over the hole as shown, making sure her elbow aligns with the top of the stamp.

4 Stamp la petite musique on a large sticky note, then cut around her silhouette with scissors. Cut out the space between her dress and hair to complete a detailed mask.

YOU WILL NEED

Clear stamps: large and small postage stamps, la petite musique

A4 orange textured card

A5 sheets of 300gsm (140lb) cold-pressed watercolour paper

Dye-based sepia archival inkpad

Dye-based plum inkpad

Dye-based cabin fever rainbow inkpad

Watercolour pencils: burnt ochre and burnt carmine

Large sticky yellow notes

Embroidery scissors

Decollage craft scissors

Make-up sponge

Brayer

Pencil

Paintbrush

Double-sided sticky tape

Scrap paper

Tip

For an authentic effect, always change the background colour of the postage stamp with a brayer or sponge – or both!

5 Place the small mask over the artwork and large mask. Use the brayer with the cabin fever rainbow inkpad, making sure you pick up red on the right-hand side of the brayer and yellow on the left-hand side. Remove some ink on scrap paper, then roll the brayer over the postage stamp area, making sure the red is at the bottom and the yellow at the top.

6 Pinch a make-up sponge into a mushroom shape and reinforce the colours at the bottom with the plum inkpad.

7 Make a mask of the large postage stamp on a sticky yellow note, taking care to cut around the serrated edge neatly. Remove the masks from the artwork and place the new mask on the artwork. Carefully trace the outline of la petite musique with the pencil.

8 Carefully stamp la petite musique in place over the new mask, using sepia ink.

9 Remove the new mask and use the burnt carmine watercolour pencil to colour her dress, and burnt ochre to colour her skin. Soften the colours with a damp brush.

10 Cut out a 5¾cm (2¼in) circle mask from a sticky yellow note and place it over her head. Replace the large postage stamp mask, then use a make-up sponge with the yellow part of the cabin fever inkpad to add colour around the mask.

11 Remove the masks and trim the artwork down to 11 x 13cm (4½ x 5¼in), using the craft scissors to get a distressed edge.

12 Use the small postage stamp with sepia ink on a 12 x 5cm (5 x 2in) strip of watercolour paper.

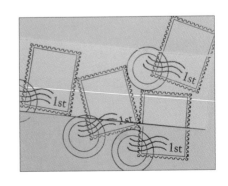

13 Add details inside the stamps with various parts of la petite musique and sepia ink.

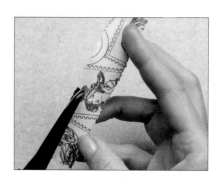

14 Use the cabin fever rainbow inkpad with the brayer to add colour to the strip, then trim it to 10 x 2cm (4 x ¾in) with the decollage craft scissors.

Tip

Whenever you are using water or watercolour pencils, be sure to use a water-resistant archival inkpad to avoid the line art bleeding.

15 Use another sheet of watercolour paper to create mounts for the artwork and strip, then attach the mounted piece to an orange card with double-sided sticky tape.

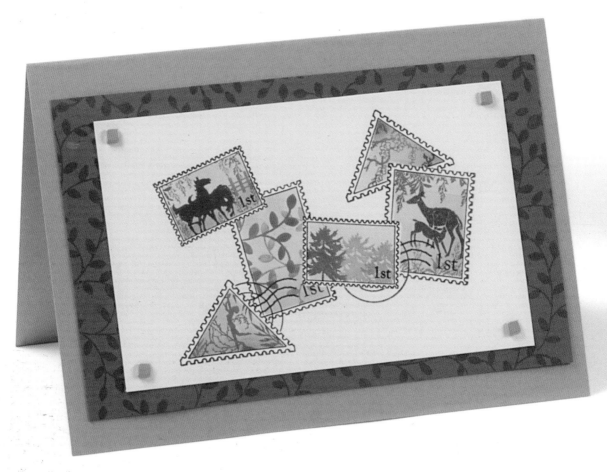

Countryside Collage

*To achieve an overlapped effect with the postage stamps,
place the front three first. Next, mask the printed stamps off
and stamp the next images into the background.*

Horses in the Paddock

The large 'postage stamp' stamp is the same as I used for the demonstration. Note that the artwork is kept within the box here.

Friends and Lovers

Four independent faux postage stamps, to create a romantic mood. The panel incorporates all the stamps used in the individual images.

Victorian Lace

This card demonstrates the versatility of a little transparent corner stamp, which is used to create a repeating pattern and a seamless lace border. This sort of pattern-building is only possible with clear stamps.

1 Cut a 14 x 9 cm (5.5 x 3.5in) piece of watercolour paper. Ink up the rose stamp and stamp the image in the bottom left-hand corner.

2 Stamp the rose on to a sticky yellow note so the image is above the side with the adhesive.

3 Use the embroidery scissors to cut the outline of the rose out of the sticky note, then apply it over the image on the watercolour paper as a mask.

4 Run strips of masking tape along each edge, covering approximately 1cm (½in) of the paper on each side.

5 Ink the Victorian corner stamp and blot it until it is a little faded, then stamp over the masking tape, allowing only the very tip of the stamp to print on the paper. Repeat this action to the left so that the second impression touches the first.

YOU WILL NEED

Clear stamps: rose, Topaze, Victorian corner

A4 sheets of 300gsm (140lb) cold-pressed watercolour paper

A4 sheet of lilac textured paper

Scrap paper

Dye-based eggplant inkpad

Low-tack masking tape

Five small gold beads

Lilac bead

10cm (4in) cord

Craft knife and cutting mat

Ruler

Embroidery scissors

Lilac colouring pencil

1/16in hole punch

Gold leafing pen

Gold wire

Sticky foam pads

Large sticky yellow notes

Double-sided sticky tape

Tip

When pattern-building with corner stamps, always practise on scrap paper to get a feel for the little stamp before you begin.

6 Repeat all around the masking tape until you reach the start.

7 Run masking tape along the tips of the top border, then ink and blot the corner stamp. Stamp the tip into the spaces between the tips of the border.

8 Work along the row, stamping into each space, then remove the masking tape, being careful not to tear the rose mask.

9 Work around the other edges in the same way, then remove the masking tape and rose mask. Use a lilac colouring pencil to add a touch of colour to the rose.

10 Cut a 3¾ x 7½cm (1.5 x 3in) piece of watercolour paper, then trim the top corners off to make a tag (see inset). Ink the Topaze stamp and stamp the tag, then use the tip of the Victorian corner stamp to stamp a border as before.

11 Colour Topaze's clothing with the lilac colouring pencil, then attach the tag to lilac paper with double-sided tape.

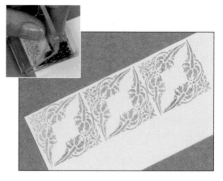

12 Cut the tag out, leaving a thin border of lilac card. Punch a hole in the tag with the hole punch, thread the cord through the hole and then thread three beads (gold, lilac and gold) on to both ends of the cord.

13 Take a 5 x 12¾cm (2 x 5in) piece of watercolour paper and ink the corner stamp. Blot it and stamp the paper in the top right corner.

14 Turn the strip round, ink the stamp, blot it and stamp next to the previous impression, creating a square (see inset). Make two more squares adjacent to the first.

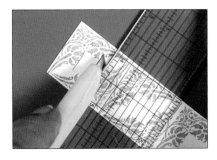

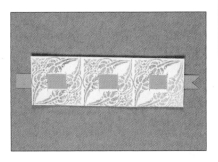

15 Use the craft knife to cut the motif out, then make a slit in the top and bottom part of the inside square of the designs as shown.

16 Cut a 0.75 x 14cm (¼ x 5½in) strip of lilac card and thread it through the slits. Make a swallow's-tail notch at one end.

17 Use the tip of your embroidery scissors to make a hole in the strip at the centre of each square (see inset). Thread a 7¾cm (3in) piece of gold wire with a bead, then poke both ends through the hole.

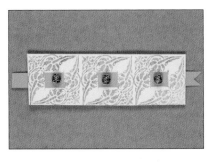

18 Twist the wire to secure the bead, and repeat the process on the other two holes.

19 Nuzzle the nib of the gold leafing pen on the edge of the motif and drag the pen along the side to edge it. Repeat the process on the main artwork.

20 Mount both pieces on lilac card (as in steps 11 and 12), then make a card from an A4 piece of watercolour paper and attach the pieces with double-sided sticky tape.

21 Attach the tag to the main artwork with sticky foam pads to complete the card.

Ornate Variations in Blue

This card illustrates several patterns using the same wonderful lace-making corner.

Three Honeysuckle Notelets

One small honeysuckle corner stamp; three delightful central motifs and a lovely border to link them to one another.

Catherine Wheel

Another variation using the Victorian corner. Here, the Catherine wheel actually rotates, turning on a brad.

VICTORIAN CARDS

by Joanna Sheen

My love for all things crafty has spanned my entire lifetime and is, I feel, the happiest hobby on earth. My specific interest is in looking back to times and standards of craftsmanship gone by. I love the gentleness of the Victorian era and the belief, so embodied in Victorian crafts, that 'if it's worth doing, it's worth doing well'. I see no point in making a card that looks as though you have not bothered to take care with your craft. I make quick cards all the time, but you should always take that extra moment or two to make sure you really are giving something that can be treasured.

I hope you will take inspiration from the projects in this section and will enjoy applying them to your card making. You do not need to follow a card exactly and make a replica – you can use papers or embellishments that you have in your workbox that will make your card unique.

The cards manufactured in those days had so many small touches of extra care – and I try to do likewise with my cards. Pretty inserts add a little something to a card. If you have scraps left, why not decorate the back of the card with a strip of toning paper and a craft sticker.

The cards shown here feature toppers or backing papers printed out on a home printer from a Victorian-themed CD. However, you can choose alternative decoupage sheets, backing papers and photographs, or search the internet for suitable images.

I hope you have many hours of fun both reading and using this section of the book and I hope you find the Victorian style as addictive as I do!

Joanna Sheen

Opposite
A selection of Victorian style greetings cards.

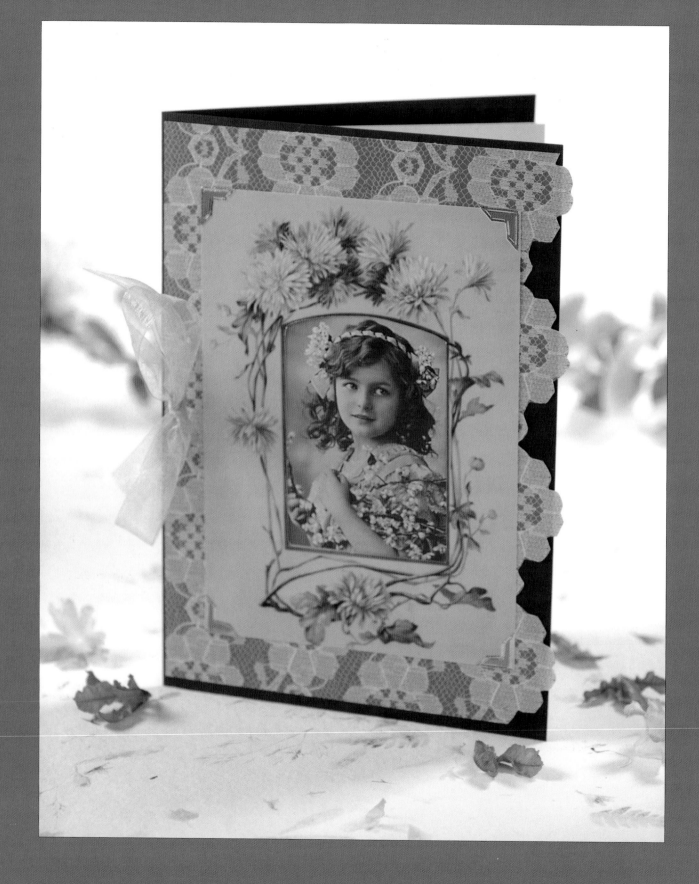

Fancy Photograph

Vintage photographs make superb subjects for cards. You can use a picture of a complete stranger just because it is beautiful or suits the message of the card, or if you are lucky enough to have a collection of old family photos, you can have one copied, save the originally carefully, and add the copy to your card. This image is from a bought set of Victorian photographs, and the lace paper is from a ready-printed pad. The flower frame was printed from a CD but you can also buy ready-printed Victorian album mounts. The flower design, lace paper and organza ribbon make this a deliciously feminine card.

YOU WILL NEED

Pink lace paper, 14.5 x 19.3cm (5¾ x 7⅝in)

Decoupage snips

Flower frame

Craft knife and cutting mat

Metal ruler

Printed photograph of girl

Maroon card blank, 14.3 x 20cm (5⅝ x 7⅞in)

Japanese screw punch or eyelet punch and hammer

Double-sided tape

Tweezers

Lilac organza ribbon

Scissors

Four gold photo corner craft stickers

1 Cut one side of the pink lace paper, following the lace pattern and using decoupage snips.

2 Cut out the centre of the flower frame using a craft knife, metal ruler and cutting mat.

3 Apply double-sided tape around the edges of the front of the photograph.

4 Mount the pink lace paper on the maroon card blank using double-sided tape. Mount the photograph and then the flower frame on top in the same way.

5 Open the card and place it on a cutting mat. Use a Japanese screw punch or an eyelet punch and hammer to make two holes for the ribbon. To use a Japanese screw punch, firmly press down into the layers of paper and card and allow the punch to twist and make the hole.

6 Use tweezers to push the end of the ribbon through the bottom hole from the inside of the card.

7 Push the other end of the ribbon through the other hole in the same way. Turn the card over and tie the ribbon in a bow. Trim the ends on the diagonal using sharp scissors.

8 Take four photo corner craft stickers, peel off the backing and place them using tweezers at the corners of the flower frame.

My Best Friend and I

This pretty vintage image is one that will please a wide variety of recipients and the colours of the sepia-toned photograph blend beautifully with the old Victorian lettering and the marbled papers.

Congratulations!

This illuminated frame has been carefully cut out and a Victorian man's photograph inserted, which together with the calligraphy-style paper and scroll would make a great card to celebrate a young man's achievement.

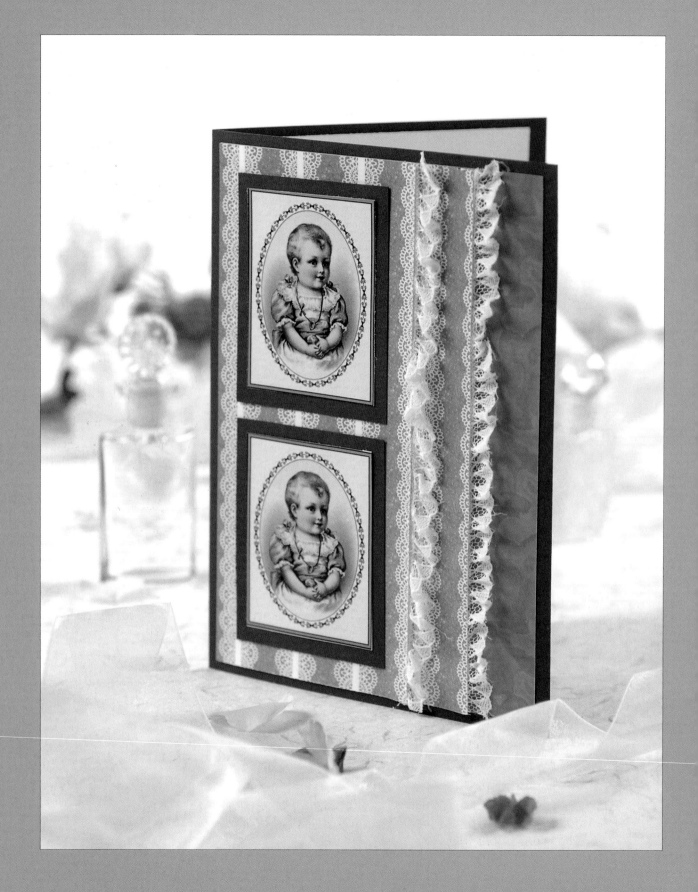

Baby Lace

One of the happiest times to celebrate is the arrival of a new baby. Mothers are often deluged with cards and flowers, gifts and callers. By making your own card rather than buying a ready-made one, you will make sure that the new mum has not only a card that is completely unique but also something she can keep and treasure forever.

The baby image and matching backing papers used here were printed from a Victorian-themed CD set, but you can choose your own.

YOU WILL NEED

Guillotine

One sheet of purple marbled paper

Two sheets of lined pink lace paper

Narrow 15mm (⁵/₈in) ruffled lace

Double-sided tape

Scissors

Sheet of maroon card

Two baby images

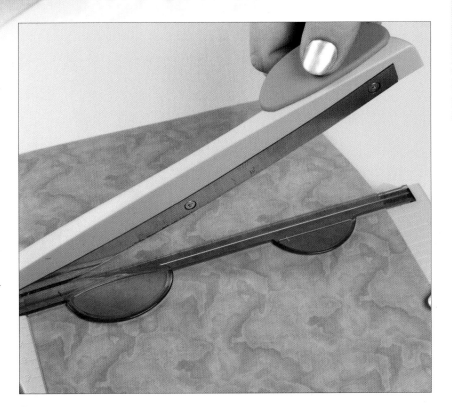

1 Use the guillotine to cut the papers to size. Cut the purple marbled paper to 13.6 x 19cm (5³/₈ x 7½in); then cut the two pieces of lace paper to 8.6 x 19cm (3³/₈ x 7½in) and 11 x 19cm (4³/₈ x 7½in).

2 Apply double-sided tape all round the back of the lace papers and remove the backing. Stick down a strip of ruffled lace on one long edge of each piece, so that the frilled edge of the lace will show from the front. Trim the lace to size.

3 Cut out the baby images. Use the guillotine to cut two pieces of maroon card, 6.5 x 8.4cm (2½ x 3⁵/₁₆in).

4 Mount the baby images on the maroon cards using double-sided tape. Mount the lace papers on to the maroon card blank, the widest first.

5 Mount the baby pictures on to the narrower piece of lace paper using double-sided tape.

Golden Baby

Wide ivory and grey lace has been wrapped around the layer of gold card and held with tape before layering on to the main card. A family baby photograph would work very successfully here too.

Baby Dreaming

The daisy design is actually a piece of decorated voile fabric, which I wrapped around a pale green piece of card. I fixed this at the back with double-sided tape and attached ruffled lace around the edge before finally attaching that layer to the base card.

Decoupage Kitten

This beautiful kitten image is made into a pretty card using decoupage techniques that give the finished project an interesting three-dimensional effect. The images I used are printed from a Victorian-themed CD set and the lace paper is from a ready-printed pad, but you could choose your own alternatives.

YOU WILL NEED

Guillotine

Two sheets of A4 brown card

One sheet of lace paper

Decoupage kitten images

Double-sided tape

Silicone glue

Craft knife

Tweezers

Decoupage snips

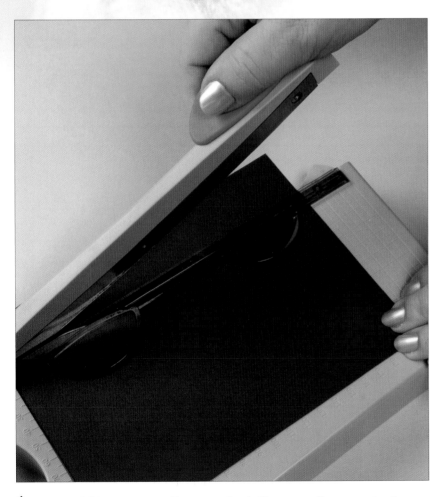

1 Score and fold an A4 piece of brown card in half. Use a guillotine to trim the folded card to 20 x 14.7cm (7⅞ x 5⅞in). Also cut a piece of the same brown card to 16.5 x 11.4cm (6½ x 4½in).

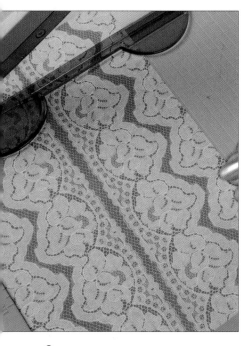

2 Cut the lace paper to 19 x 13.7cm (7½ x 5³⁄₈in).

3 Take the four kitten images and cut them out as shown, using decoupage snips.

4 Apply double-sided tape to the backs of the lace paper and the piece of brown card.

5 Peel off the backing from the double-sided tape and mount the lace paper and the brown card on the main card. Apply double-sided tape to the full kitten image and mount this on top.

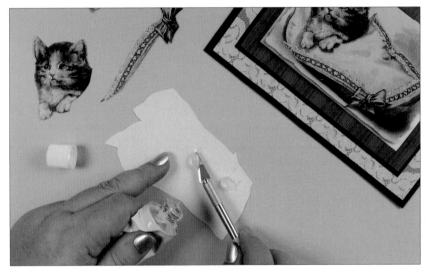

6 Apply silicone glue to the back of the next kitten image (top right of step 3) and mount this on the card. Next, apply silicone glue to the back of the next image (bottom left of step 3). Use a craft knife to help you apply blobs of silicone glue. Always clean your craft knife immediately when using it with silicone glue, or use a cocktail stick instead.

7 Apply silicone glue to the backs of the final pieces and place these on the card using tweezers. Leave them to dry for at least half an hour and preferably overnight before putting the card in the post.

Exotic Birds

Birds are popular with both men and women, so this makes an excellent card for a whole range of people. The birds are decoupaged and the picture mounted on several layers of cool blue marbled papers. The black edges bring out the colours beautifully and add contrast to the overall design.

He's Bigger Than Me!

This delightful vintage image of two dogs makes a wonderful focal point and shows how effectively a Victorian image can be decoupaged. The colour toning of the marbled papers, gold and brown card gives a very satisfying result.

FAIRY CARDS

by Judy Balchin

I have literally been 'away with the fairies' while writing this section and have enjoyed every magical minute of it. The end of every day has found me covered in glitter and usually sporting a few gold and silver sequins as I wander round my local supermarket. This has naturally raised a few comments amongst my friends and family. So at last, here are my vintage fairy cards. The fairies have all faithfully promised to cast their tiny spells as you work. I hope that by the time you have finished making the cards in this section, you too will be away with the fairies... and proud of it! Have fun,

Judy

Snow Fairy

Bring this thoughtful Snow Fairy to life by including icy silver sequins and stars into the central shaker panel. All the images in this section were printed from a CD, but there are also plenty of vintage fairy images available on the internet. Cool colours are used to reflect the beauty of the fairy's frozen world.

1 Use spray glue to attach the larger piece of pale blue glitter card to the base card and the rainbow card on top.

You will need

Fairy images

Lilac card measuring 13 x 15cm (5 x 6in) when folded in half

Pale blue glitter card: 12 x 14.5cm (4¾ x 5¾in) and 8 x 10.5cm (3 x 4in)

Rainbow card 11 x 13.5cm (4¼ x 5¼in)

White card 8 x 10.5cm (3 x 4in)

Acetate 7 x 9.5cm (2¾ x 3¾in)

Sticky foam tape

Silver star gems and sequins

Iridescent sequins

Pale blue organza ribbon

Scalpel

Ruler

Spray glue

Crafter's glue

2 Print out the 6 x 8.5cm (2¼ x 3¼in) fairy image on your computer and cut it out. Glue it to the middle of the piece of white card with crafter's glue.

Opposite:
The finished card. Print a smaller fairy image to use on a matching gift tag.

3 Press lengths of foam tape round the white border, trimming them neatly to fit.

4 Place the gems and sequins within the recess and gently remove the backing tape on the foam strips.

5 Press the acetate on to the foam frame.

6 Measure and draw a 1cm (½in) border on to the back of the smaller piece of pale blue glitter card. Cut out the aperture using the scalpel.

7 Press the glitter card frame on top of the acetate.

8 Glue the shaker panel to the middle of the base card with crafter's glue.

9 Use crafter's glue to attach a ribbon bow to the top left corner of the frame.

10 Decorate the card with stars.

Your finished Snow Fairy, surrounded by her icy embellishments.

Nature Fairy

Gold and silver sequin stars and leaves are inserted into this shaker card to mirror this Nature Fairy as she listens to the birds. The frame is decorated with flower sequins and gems and a backing panel of floral paper echoes the theme. The simple matching gift tag uses just one flower embellishment as a central motif.

Dream Fairy

Blue and silver sets the theme for this Dream Fairy as she sits watching the moonlit sea. The shaker panel uses small blue and silver sequins as decoration with a surrounding frame of glitter card. Backed with a panel of torn handmade paper and decorated with a sprinkling of tiny stars, this card will make sure that this fairy's dreams will come true. The matching gift tag uses a smaller picture version of the main card.

Frolicking Fairies

Iridescent and pastel glitter papers are used to mirror this delicate picture of Frolicking Fairies. Sparkling stars dance in the shaker panel as the fairies swoop and dive.

Forest Fairy

There are some beautiful rubber stamps on the market. Take time to find your perfect fairy stamp. Simply stamped and gently coloured, the Forest Fairy drifts gently within her painted and embossed panels. A torn handmade paper surround reminds her of her woodland home.

1 Paint the two pieces of thick card with jade paint. When dry, add random streaks of pale green and brown paint.

2 When dry, stamp the larger piece of card with scroll patterns using the scroll rubber stamp and an embossing pad.

3 Place it on to a sheet of scrap paper and sprinkle it with gold embossing powder. Shake off the excess powder on to the paper.

Opposite:
The tag is made with the same techniques as the card, using a Funstamps F-C18 eight pointed star rubber stamp.

4 Heat the scroll pattern with a heat tool until the powder melts and looks metallic.

You will need

2 pieces of thick card:
  6 x 13cm (2⅜ x 5in) and
  4 x 9.5cm (1½ x 3¾in)

Gold card 18 x 22cm (7 x 8¾in)

Green card 7 x 14cm (2¾ x 5½in)

Green handmade paper 18 x 11cm
  (7 x 4⅜in)

Acrylic paints: pale green, jade green
  and brown

Fairy rubber stamp:
  Personal Impressions P735G

Scroll pattern rubber stamp:
  Penny Black 2636K

Black inkpad

Embossing pad and gold
  embossing powder

Heat tool

Small green sequin stars

Coloured pencils – pale green, blue
  and flesh coloured

Paintbrush

Spray glue

Scrap paper

Strong clear glue

Crafter's glue

5   Use a black inkpad to stamp a fairy on to the smaller piece of painted card and leave until dry.

6   Colour the stamped fairy with coloured pencils.

7   Glue the fairy panel on top of the painted scroll panel with clear glue.

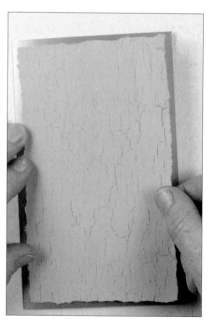

8   Decorate the area around the fairy with sequin stars, securing them with crafter's glue and moving them into place with the paintbrush.

9   Tear a 5mm (¼in) strip from each edge of the green handmade paper.

10   Score and fold the gold card down the middle and spray glue the handmade paper to the centre.

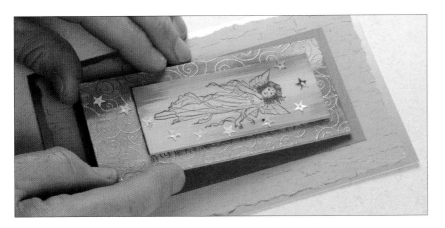

11 Glue the green card on top, again using spray glue; then attach the scroll and fairy panels to the middle of the green card with clear glue.

Fragile Forest Fairy makes the perfect centrepiece for this delicate card.

Music Fairy

Sing along with your Music Fairy (the stamp is Personal Impressions P224F) as she rests gently in her pastel world. A music stamp (Personal Impressions P593R) is used as the back panel. Sequin stars are used to cascade across the finished card. The matching gift tag has a stamp-embossed star (Funstamps F-C18) as its central motif.

Nightshade Fairy

Blue and green paints and papers are used to create this night-loving fairy (the image is Personal Impressions P736G). The same techniques are used as in the project, substituting a script rubber stamp (Sirius Hobby Stamp 'Tekst') for the back panel. Small purple stars decorate her as she drifts through the twilight.

Dancing Fairy

Cream, lilac and pink paints are used to paint the backing panels giving this fairy (made using Personal Impressions P243E) a perfect stage on which to perform her magic. The base card uses pastel colours with small pink and silver stars for decoration. The back panel uses the same stamp (Sirius Hobby Stamp 'Tekst') as the Nightshade Fairy.

CELTIC CARDS

by Paula Pascual

I couldn't say when it all started, but my fascination with all things Celtic – whether it be design, symbolism, music, history or art – goes back a long way, to when I was a child on the Spanish island of Majorca. The intrinsic beauty of the Celts is eternal, and goes beyond the barriers of time. Being able to combine it with my biggest craft passion, papercrafting, is a fantastic opportunity for me.

When I am teaching or demonstrating cardmaking, people often ask me to share my ideas on how to make cards for the men in their life. I tried to keep this in mind when I was designing the cards for this section, and therefore included a number of cards with a more masculine appeal.

In the project on page 85 I have provided a template from the book *Celtic Designs* by Courtney Davis, published in the *Design Source Book* series by Search Press. This book, together with *Celtic Knotwork Designs* by Elaine Hill, *Celtic Borders and Motifs* by Lesley Davis and *The Complete Book of Celtic Designs*, all published by Search Press, represent a rich source of designs, patterns and inspiration.

The best thing I can say to you is this: have fun experimenting with all the techniques and ideas in this section, and I hope they will inspire you to create beautiful Celtic designs of your own.

Silver Gate

This gatefold card involves three different techniques for achieving some wonderful effects: stencilling with brass stencils, embossing and chalking. I have used two embossing methods: the first uses embossing tools to create a raised image, and the second uses embossing paste, which is specially designed to be used with brass stencils and dries to a metallic finish.

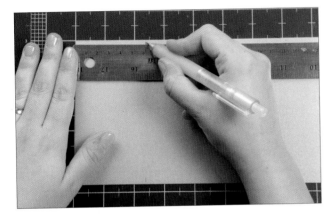

1 To make a gatefold card, first place the silver card on a cutting mat and align it with the grid so that the longer edges run widthways. Measure 6cm (2¼in) in from each edge along the top and the bottom, and mark with a pencil.

2 Fold in each side and strengthen the fold by running the folder firmly along their length.

YOU WILL NEED

One sheet of silver card, 24 x 12cm (9½ x 4¾in)

Small piece of dark blue card, at least 10cm (4in) square

Small piece of silver card, at least 10cm (4in) square

Cutting mat

Retractable pencil or sharp pencil

Metal ruler

Circular Celtic brass stencil, e.g. Dreamweaver, LL380

Rectangular Celtic brass stencil, e.g. Marianne Designs, CT6004

Low-tack tape

Silver embossing paste

Spatula

Circle cutting system

Double-sided adhesive tape

Bone folder

Greaseproof paper

Light blue chalk

Small foam eye-shadow applicator

Eraser

Embossing tool

3 Attach the circular brass stencil to the piece of blue card using four strips of low-tack tape, one along each edge of the stencil.

4 Spread silver embossing paste over the back of the design using a spatula. Smooth it over so that the paste fills the design.

5 Carefully remove three of the four low-tack tape strips.

6 Gently lift up the stencil, leaving it secured on one side, revealing the design underneath. Remove the stencil completely, clean it, and allow the paste to dry.

7 Meanwhile, attach the rectangular brass stencil to the front of the right-hand flap of the card blank using low-tack tape.

8 Open up the card and rub firmly over the back of the stencil using the end of a bone folder wrapped in greaseproof paper. The indented design will gradually appear.

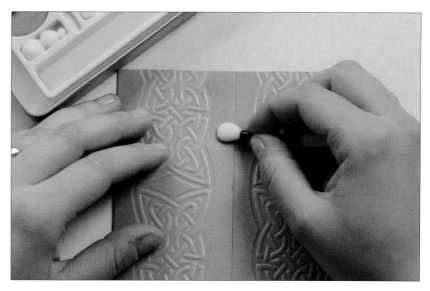

9 Using an embossing tool, press firmly over the indentations to deepen them and strengthen the design. Repeat on the left-hand flap of the card.

10 Use blue chalk applied with a small foam eye-shadow applicator to the front of the card, down the sides of the design.

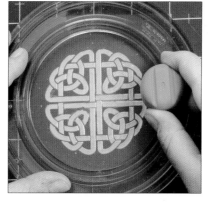

11 Remove excess chalk with an eraser for a more subtle finish.

12 Working on a cutting mat, use a circle cutting system to cut around the design. Leave a wide blue border.

13 Cut out a silver circle slightly larger than the blue. Attach the blue circle to the silver using double-sided tape.

14 Attach the motif to the left-hand flap on the front of the card.

For the card below I used a stencil (Marianne Design, CT6004) as a simple embossed background and left it plain. On a red card I used white embossing paste over a circular brass stencil (Dreamweaver, LL326 'Hearts Knot'). Once the paste is dry, you can colour it with any coloured chalks. Alternatively, you can use silver embossing paste.

To achieve the matt black finish on this card I have used black embossing paste with a circular brass stencil (Dreamweaver, LL520 'Love Knot'), which works well in combination with the rubber-stamped circular border (Heritage Rubber Stamp Co., Celt6XLS3).

You can also use brass stencils as a cutting guide to create apertures, as I have done here with this Marianne Design, CT6002. First I embossed the image on to white paper, then I coloured it with green chalks and finally I cut out the petal-shaped details with a craft knife. To make the most of the aperture I used thick (220gsm) vellum for the green card blank and red 100gsm vellum on top, which allows the light to show through.

This cross motif is perfect for an Easter, christening or sympathy card. Here I have embossed the card using a brass stencil (Dreamweaver, LG647 'Celtic Cross') and coloured it with chalks, for which it is best to use non-glossy card. I then trimmed away the centre aperture and the edges so that I could raise the image with 3D foam pads.

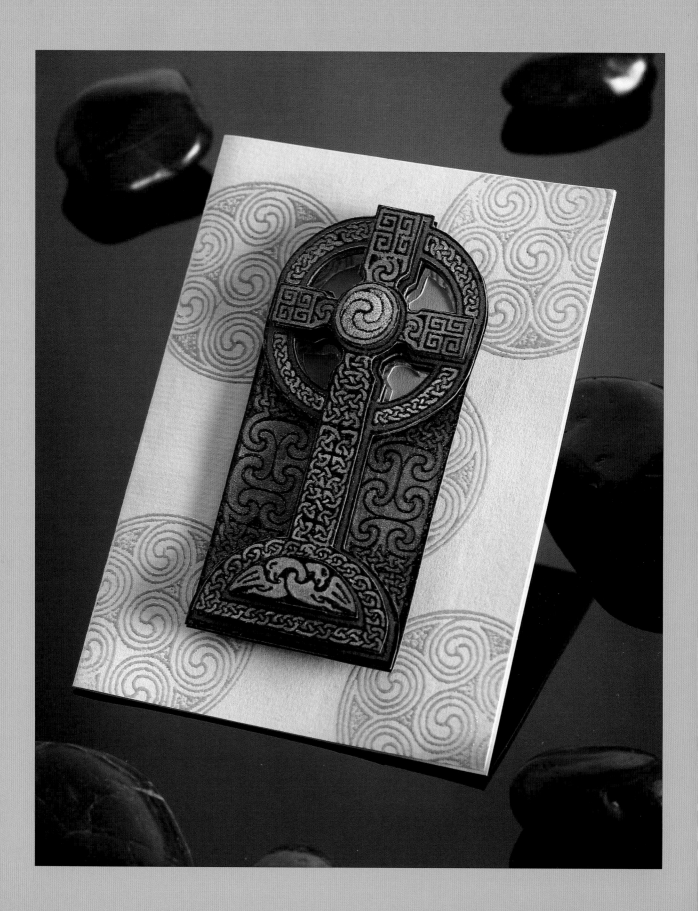

Emerald Cross

This project takes your stamping to another level: it involves layering several images to produce a three-dimensional (decoupaged) effect. Beautiful pearlescent watercolour paint, made from pigment powder and gum arabic, is used to colour the images, and a subtle patterned background created by heat embossing together with a tiny amount of silver glitter placed in the centre of the cross complete the card.

Tip

Some pigment powders already contain gum arabic. For these, just add one part water to two parts powder to create the watercolour paint.

1 To make the pearlescent watercolour paint, mix two parts pearlescent pigment powder with one part gum arabic using a spatula. Leave the mixture to dry overnight.

YOU WILL NEED

Light green card blank, 10.5 x 14.5cm (4¼ x 5¾in)

Green pearlescent pigment powder

Gum arabic (fixative)

Spatula

Small plastic container with a lid

One sheet of A4 dark green card

Celtic cross rubber stamp, e.g. Heritage Rubber Stamp Co., Celt5XLS1

Circular Celtic spiral rubber stamp, e.g. Heritage Rubber Stamp Co., Celt3XLS4

Watermark inkpad

Dark green and light green embossing powders

Heat gun

Water brush

Craft knife

Cutting mat

Low-tack tape

Retractable pencil or sharp pencil

3D foam pads

PVA glue in a fine-tip applicator

Fine white glitter

2 Stamp the Celtic cross design four times on the dark green card using the watermark inkpad.

3 Cover the images with the dark green embossing powder, tip the excess back into the pot, and heat with a heat gun until the powder turns shiny.

4 Using a water brush and the green pearlescent paint, colour the panel on each side of the cross in one of the images.

5 Choose a second image, and colour the circle behind the cross.

 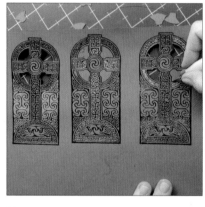

6 In the third image, colour the cross itself, including the border around its base, and in the fourth colour the entwined birds and the circular spiral design in the centre.

7 Working on a cutting mat, use a craft knife to cut out the shapes between the cross and the circle in the first and second images. These will form the first two layers of the three-dimensional design.

8 From the third image, create the third layer by cutting out the cross and its base, and from the fourth (the top layer of the design) cut out the spiral that lies in the centre of the cross and the entwined birds within its base.

10 Cover the stamped images with light green embossing powder. Tip the excess powder back into the pot. Use the heat gun to heat the image, holding it 10cm (4in) from the surface. Stop heating as soon as the embossing powder melts and becomes shiny. Position the bottom layer of the Celtic cross design accurately on the front of the card and attach it using low-tack tape. Outline the shapes within the top of the cross using a pencil.

9 Stamp the spiral design four or five times in a random pattern over the front of the card blank using the watermark inkpad.

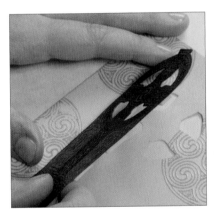

11 Remove the Celtic cross, open out the card and place it on a cutting mat. Cut out the shapes marked on the card using a craft knife, cutting just outside the pencil lines.

12 Place 3D foam pads on the back of the first Celtic cross and attach it to the card, aligning the cut-out shapes.

13 Build up the layers in the order in which they were cut out. Secure each layer using 3D foam pads.

14 Apply PVA glue, using a fine-tip applicator, to the spiral design in the centre of the cross.

15 Sprinkle the spiral design with fine white glitter and tip off the excess to complete the card.

For this intricate cross I chose a blue theme and used good quality felt-tip pens to colour it in. I used an image from the Heritage Rubber Stamp Co., Celt2XLS2, and embossed it in silver twice. For the frame I used the stamp Celt5XLS3, also from the Heritage Rubber Stamp Co., and trimmed it to the inside edge.

For the blue, circular design I used watercolour paper as the base for the stamped and embossed image, for which I used a stamp from the Heritage Rubber Stamp Co., Celt4XLS4. This created texture on the embossed image, reminiscent of the movement of water. I also added some fine white glitter, as described in the project.

A monochromatic card is perfect for a wedding; just change the colour if gold is not your favourite. I use two stamps that have the same image but in different sizes – Heritage Rubber Stamp Co., Celt3XLS12 and CeltLS15. I use some gold ribbon on the back to add more texture. Once trimmed, the stamped images are attached with 3D foam pads for a three-dimensional effect.

For the card below I used the Heritage Rubber Stamp Co., Celt4XLS8 rubber stamp and purple embossing powder, then coloured in the image with felt-tip pens and finished it off with glitter. Velvet ribbon always has a very special feel about it and adds extra texture to the card.

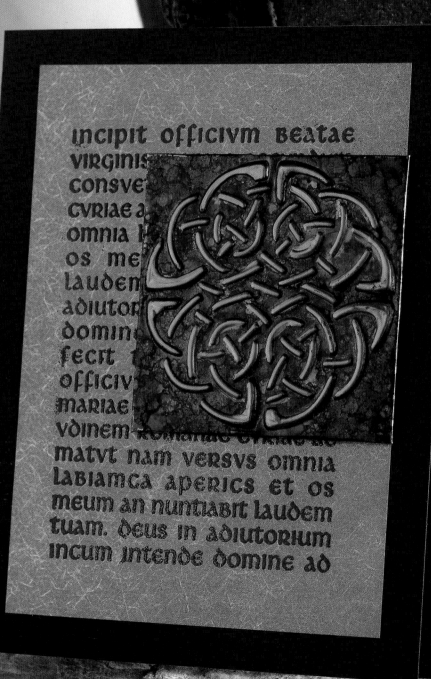

incipit officivm beatae
virginis
consve
cvriae a
omnia l
os me
laudem
adiutor
domine
fecit
officiv
mariae
vdinem
matvt nam versvs omnia
labiamca aperics et os
meum an nuntiabit laudem
tuam. deus in adiutorium
incum intende domine ad

Copper Script

Using thin metal sheets may be daunting at first, but it is actually a very easy and rewarding medium to work with. Here I have embossed a raised design on to the metal using a brass stencil, and coloured it using alcohol inks. These dry to a rich, jewel-like finish that works perfectly to create the ancient feel of this card.

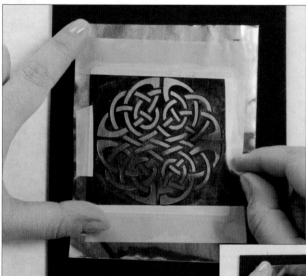

1 Attach the circular brass stencil to the lightweight copper sheet using low-tack tape. Place it on a foam mat.

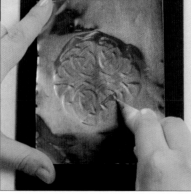

2 Turn the metal over and rub over the stencil with a large stump tool to reveal the design.

YOU WILL NEED

One burgundy card blank,
12.5 x 16cm (5 x 6¼in)

Lightweight copper sheet,
approximately 10cm (4in) square

One large sheet of scrap paper

One small piece of copper metallic paper, at least 12 x 15cm (4¾ x 6in)

Circular Celtic brass stencil, e.g.
Dreamweaver, LL520

Large background script rubber stamp, e.g. Heritage Rubber Stamp Co., Celt6XLS1

Low-tack tape

Foam mat

Large and fine stump tools

Round-ended and pointed embossing tools

Black embossing paste

Palette knife

Piece of thin chipboard

Scissors

Alcohol inks in four different shades (reds, browns and oranges)

Alcohol ink applicator and blending solution

Cotton bud

Watermark inkpad

Heat gun

Dusty pink embossing powder

Adhesive roller

Large glue dots

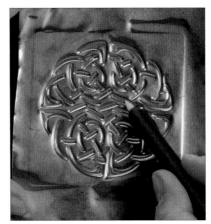

4 Repeat using a pointed embossing tool to accentuate the design further and bring out the fine detail.

3 Strengthen the design by going over the indentations with a round-ended embossing tool.

5 Finally, go over the indentations again with a fine stump tool to smooth them.

6 Turn the metal over and remove the stencil.

7 Turn the metal over again, and spread black embossing paste over the back of the design using a palette knife. The paste is forced into the indentations, which helps to hold them in place and prevents them from being flattened.

8 Cut a square piece of thin chipboard just slighly larger than the stencilled design. Attach the board to the back of the design using an adhesive roller, and trim off the corners of the metal sheet.

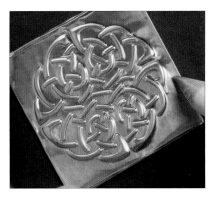

9 Fold the sides of the metal over the chipboard square, turn the design over so that it is face up, and flatten the edges and sharpen the corners using the large stump tool.

10 Place a drop of each of the four alcohol inks on the pad of the applicator so that they merge together.

11 Dab the ink firmly over the surface of the design.

12 Add more ink to the applicator and apply another layer of colour to create a mottled effect. Repeat this as many times as you wish, then leave to dry.

13 Use alcohol ink blending solution applied with a cotton bud to remove the ink from the raised parts of the design. If you accidentally remove ink from the background, simply apply more ink.

14 Cut a piece of copper metallic card so that it is 1cm (½in) smaller all round than the card blank. Apply the watermark inkpad to the background stamp, and stamp the image on to the copper paper.

15 Emboss the stamped image using dusty rose embossing powder.

16 Attach the stamped copper paper to the card blank using the adhesive roller, then attach the embossed metal design using large glue dots. Off-set it so that it is positioned slightly higher than the centre line and aligned with the right-hand edge of the copper paper.

For the tall card below right, use a black metal sheet and emboss it using a brass stencil (Marianne Design, CT6004), then apply alcohol inks on top. Trim the edges and use a tracing wheel or a piercing tool to add a border each side of the metal embossed image.

A cool look for copper, shown on the card below left, is to heat it, which causes the copper to change colour. The best way to do this is to emboss the copper first and then apply the heat with a hand-held heat gun – the type used by chefs is better for this than craft heat guns, as they produce more heat. Once the colour has changed and the metal has cooled down, apply embossing paste to the back and attach the metal to the card. Finish the card off with a crystal in the centre.

To make the card shown below left, use a silver metal sheet and emboss it using a brass stencil (Marianne Design, CT6007). To create the matt effect, use a metal brush and brush over the top of the metal with circular motions. Apply alcohol inks on top. Attach the motif to a piece of card stamped with a background image (here I have used Heritage Rubber Stamp Co., Celt6XLS2) and attach this to a card blank, overhanging one edge.

Try stamping on to metal using a solvent inkpad. On the card shown below I stamped on to silver metal sheet with white ink and let it dry for a couple of minutes. I then embossed the metal border using a mould, which I used in exactly the same way as a brass stencil. Finally I glued both the border and the central motif on to the card using strong adhesive.

Spiral of Light

When it comes to adding impact to your cards, there is nothing as fun and as amazing as alcohol inks. These beautiful inks allow you to colour any non-porous surface, and will dry instantly. The inks blend together even when dry, allowing you continually to add different amounts of various colours until the desired effect is achieved. The addition of tiny patches of artificial gold leaf makes it glimmer and sparkle as it catches the light, enhancing the jewel-like quality of this card.

Template for the design, actual size. (Reproduced from Celtic Designs *by Courtney Davis)*

YOU WILL NEED

Dark green pearlescent card blank, 10.5cm (4¼in) square

One piece of black card, at least 9cm (3½in) square

One piece of gold metallic card, at least 9cm (3½in) square

One sheet of A4 transparency paper

One sheet of A4 photocopier paper

One sheet of scrap paper

Alcohol inks in various golds and greens

Alcohol ink applicator

Alcohol ink blending solution

Cotton bud

Pinpoint roller glue pen

Small pieces of imitation gold leaf

Adhesive roller

PVA glue in a fine-tip applicator

Sharp scissors

1 Make several copies of the design on an A4 sheet of transparency paper. Do this by first copying the design several times on to a sheet of white photocopier paper, and then copying this on to transparency paper.

2 Choose the best quality image, cut it out and place it face down on a piece of scrap paper. Place drops of alcohol ink in various shades of gold and green so that they blend together on the pad.

3 Stamp firmly over the back of the design. Build up several layers of colour, turning the design over regularly and varying the inks used to achieve the required effect.

4 Remove the ink from the tiny circles on the design using alcohol ink blending solution applied with a cotton bud.

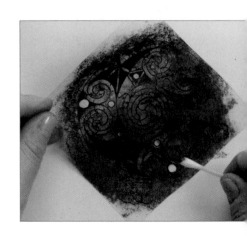

5 Apply a thin coat of low-tack glue to each circle using a pinpoint roller glue pen.

6 Lay small pieces of imitation gold leaf over each circle.

7 Turn the design face up and trim carefully around the outside using a sharp pair of scissors. Retain the outer black line.

8 Trim the black card so that it is approximately 1cm (½in) smaller all round than the card blank, and cut a piece of gold metallic card just slightly smaller than this. Mount the two pieces of card on the card blank using the adhesive roller.

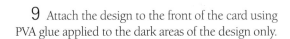

9 Attach the design to the front of the card using PVA glue applied to the dark areas of the design only.

To create the intricate pattern on the card below is really easy. Make two copies of your chosen design on acetate and then apply alcohol inks to both of them. Remove the inks from the circles. Once dried, trim the designs to size and attach them on top of glitter paper so that it shows through the gaps.

For the card on the right, I matched the colours of the patterned paper with the alcohol inks, and applied transparent glitter glue to highlight the pattern on the main motif. After the glitter glue had dried (it takes a while for glitter glue to dry on acetate), I trimmed around the motif and attached it to the card.

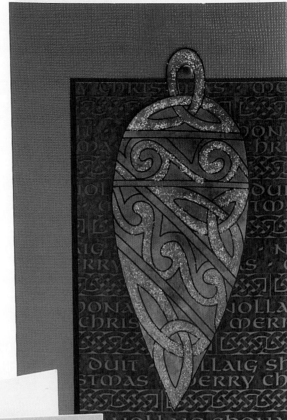

The design below left is very similar to the project; the difference is that the clear gaps are left clear so that the texture of the card underneath shows through. Finish the card by stamping an image in each corner using gold ink.

For a card with a difference, position the main motif over the top edge of the card, as on the design shown below right. Just make sure there is an envelope large enough for the entire card! Stamp the frame (Heritage Rubber Stamp Co., Celt4XLS3) on to turquoise card and trim around it, glue a piece of silver paper on the back and then attach the complete motif to the card. Apply alcohol inks to the peacock and attach it to the inside of the frame.

BEADED CARDS

by Patricia Wing

There are so many techniques you can use for cardmaking, and using beads, gems and lace with pricking and embossing techniques will considerably add to your repertoire.

There is a wealth of templates available for pricking out and stencils for embossing, to help create that extra special card. Most templates and stencils are a pleasure to work with, as someone has already created the design – you only have to follow the pattern, so pricking out or embossing could not be easier. If you cannot find the exact templates or stencils shown in this section, choose alternatives in similar shapes and sizes.

Stitching on beads adds another dimension, as do all the lovely gems. Beautiful lace will also complement the beadwork and you will be surprised at the originality you can achieve by cutting out designs from within the lace.

The Victorians produced some extraordinarily beautiful cards, which form an important part of the heritage they bequeathed to us. Equally, the cards you create could become future family heirlooms that your family will cherish in years to come.

Keep an eye open for inexpensive jewellery – old earrings and brooches often have attractive glass gems that will enhance your work and make it unique. You can find all sorts of things in charity shops, and locally I visit an auction house where boxes of broken jewellery and oddments can yield a treasure-trove of embellishments for my cards!

Pat Wing

Opposite
These cards show some of the effects that can be created using beads, gems, pricking and embossing techniques and lace in your card making.

Cameo Card

This is a very simple card to produce using just two pricking templates, beads and thread. The subtle shades of the materials used give it an elegant, period feel. You can change the colours of the cameo and everything else to suit your personal taste.

1 Tape the pricking template to the inside front of the cream card and begin pricking the design using a pricking tool and mat.

2 Finish pricking the border and close the cream card to reveal the design.

YOU WILL NEED

A5 pink160gsm (90lb) pastel card

Cream card blank, folded size 124 x 162mm (4^7/$_8$ x 6^3/$_8$in)

Pricking templates PR0507 and PR0509

Pencil

Masking tape

Fine scissors

Needle and thread

Pearl seed beads

Pink cameo

Fine-tipped PVA glue applicator and cocktail stick

2mm (^{1}/$_{16}$in) pearl beads

Pricking tool and mat

3D foam squares

3 Tape the oval template on to the pink card, pencil round it and cut it out.

Opposite

The finished card shows the two styles of pricking: from the back, creating the raised border, and from the front, giving a softer look – a perfect base on which to sew beads for a neat yet stylish finish.

4 Prick part of the design using a pricking tool and mat.

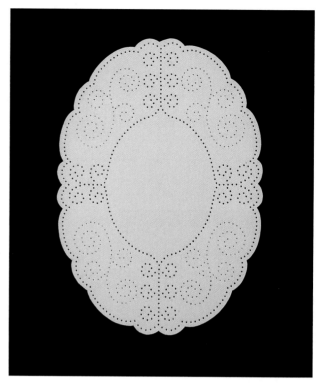

5 Remove the template, turn the card over and prick the rest of the design from the other side to create a partly raised, partly flat pattern as shown.

6 Sew on the pearl seed beads using back stitch.

7 Place 3D foam squares on the back of the pricked oval and peel off the backing.

8 Stick the oval down in the centre of the pricked cream card blank.

9 Stick the cameo in the centre of the card using PVA glue.

10 Glue a row of 2mm ($^1/_{16}$in) pearl beads around the edge of the cameo using PVA glue and a cocktail stick.

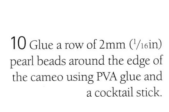

11 Use the fine-tipped PVA glue applicator to place tiny dots of glue outside the circle of pearls. Use a cocktail stick dipped in glue to pick up and place seed beads as shown.

Top left: Draw round the edge of template PR0529 on pale green parchment, cut out the shape and prick out the raised design from the reverse. Mount this on to gold card and stick to a basic card 125 x 160mm (5 x 6¼in). Now place template PR0507 on the front of some ivory card and prick out part of the design as shown. Make the flowers by using template PR0558 to prick out the pattern and then stitching on pearl beads. Use tube beads for the stems and gems to complete the flowers. Mount the stitched design on to blue then gold cards leaving narrow borders showing and fix the gold card on to the pricked green parchment.

Bottom left: Using part of template PR0529, prick out to show the raised effect on the cream card. Emboss round the edge of the envelope template and cut this out. Use part of stencil 5802S to emboss the top flap. Finish with silk ribbon and gems.

Opposite, top: Take a cream 125mm (5in) square card blank and prick out the corners from the reverse to give the raised effect. Stick amber gems in each corner. Using template PR0536, first prick out the bottom half of the design and draw around the scallop edge, then turn the template and repeat this for the top half of the design before cutting out as shown. Place on to a circle of deep cream card. Next make up the centre flower using template PR0509, mount this on to a cream circle and embellish with the daisy.

Opposite, far right: The overall size of this bookmark is 60 x 185mm (2³/₈ x 7¼in). Start with a piece of blue/green card and a piece of cream card this size. Using template PR0509, prick out and scallop the edge of the cream card and stick this to the blue/green backing which has had the corners cut with corner scissors. Next cut the inner card, trim its corners and prick it using template PR0558 to take the beads and gems.

Lilac and Lace

Lilac stitched beads and parchment blend together so well to complement a selected piece of white lace. The corners of the lightly textured card are embossed to add further elegance.

1 Tape the embossing stencil on the light box.

2 Open the card blank and tape it in place as shown. Emboss the corner using the embossing tool. Emboss each of the other three corners in the same way.

YOU WILL NEED

Light box

Cream card blank, folded size 120mm x 175mm (4¾ x 6⅞in)

A5 cream card

Stencils 5802S and EF8013

Template PR0507

Masking tape

Lilac seed beads

Needle and thread

Lilac parchment

Pricking tool and mat

Embossing tool

Pencil

Fine scissors

Piece of lace

Fine-tipped PVA glue applicator

Double-sided tape

The card with the four corners embossed.

3 Tape the stencil on the front of the card with the pricking out design in the corner, just inside the embossed design. Prick out the design in each corner, using a pricking tool and mat.

4 Thread a needle and tape the end to the back of the card, then come up through a hole, pick up a bead and secure it by going down a hole. Sew on all the beads in this way.

5 Using the same pricking out design on purple parchment, prick out the pattern four times.

6 Using the prick marks as a guide, cut out teardrop shapes from the purple parchment.

7 Using your scissors to pick up the teardrop shapes, place them inside the beaded shapes.

8 Apply masking tape to the parts of the oval template that will not be used.

9 Stick the stencil on to lilac parchment. Turn the parchment over and run the medium embossing tool around the top half of the template.

10 Realign the template ready to do the bottom half.

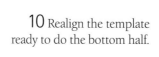

11 Run the embossing tool around the bottom half.

12 Remove the template and cut around the outside of the embossed line.

13 Stick the stencil to the A5 cream card and pencil round the top edge.

14 Prick the last hole on each side as shown.

15 Realign the template using the pricked holes as a guide and pencil around the bottom edge.

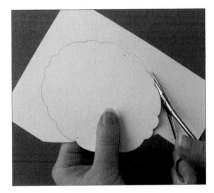

16 Cut out the shape.

17 Reapply the template and lightly prick the edge.

18 Stitch on lilac beads around the border as described in step 4.

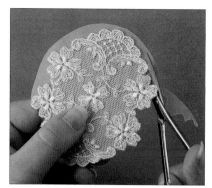

19 Cut out the lace motif.

20 Mount the lace on to lilac parchment using dots of glue behind heavy areas of lace. Trim away the edges.

21 Mount the lace and parchment on to the beaded cream card using double-sided tape.

22 Mount these on to the lilac parchment oval in the same way.

23 Mount the artwork on to the main card.

Top left: Use part of template PRO505 to prick out the basic pattern for stitching, then use the flower design in the corner of the template to make the two flowers in the centre of the card. Stitch the outline in pale turquoise and ivory beads before gluing the appropriate beads into the patterns. Cut out and stick on pale turquoise lace before adding the final bead embellishments.

Top right: Using template PRO554 for the centre and PRO559 for the corners, I have pricked out the simple but effective design you see stitched with pale yellow seed beads. Twelve large, pale, amber flat-backed teardrops are glued on and cut-out lace is repeated in the four corners. The central lace flower has been enhanced with tiny pale yellow beads.

Bottom left: Template PRO558 is used to prick out raised patterns at the sides and a flat pattern for stitching on beads in the centre. Two strips of white lace backed with pink parchment are then laid between the patterns.

Bottom right: The square card has embossed corners from stencil 5802S. The design is pricked out from template PRO536 after first embossing the edge of the template in to the card. Pale amber seed beads are stitched on, flat-backed pearls are added and the white seed beads are glued into the amber patterns. The lace is added last.

CARDS FOR ALL OCCASIONS

by Joanna Sheen

Welcome to my world of cards. Cards, flowers and crafting have been lifetime passions for me. We have been running our craft company for thirty years now so I make no apologies for believing that creating things makes an important contribution to the world. Handmade items show that you care and that you have given the most precious of all gifts: your time. Some of the cards in this section are simple and great for beginners. Once you are happy with these, try some of the more complex cards, and if you fancy the rewards of making more challenging cards, there are some really stunning examples for you to make. There are also lots of ideas to fill you with inspiration!

I hope you will enjoy exploring this section and pausing to look at the pretty photographs. I hope you will also find many of the hints and tips come in handy when you get stuck for inspiration. Happy cardmaking!

Moving Day

I love playing with shrink plastic. Once you have got over any initial panic – as it often behaves in an unexpected fashion – then you'll love it too!

1 Fold the white pearl card in half using the bone folder and scoring tool, then use the guillotine to trim it to 21 x 23cm (8¼ x 9in). Cut a 19 x 21cm (7½ x 8¼in) piece of gold card and use double-sided tape to mount it on top of the card. Cut a 17.5 x 20.5cm (6⅞ x 8in) piece of pale coral card and mount that on top of the gold card.

YOU WILL NEED

One 42 x 30cm (16½ x 12in) sheet of white pearl card

One 30 x 21cm (12 x 8¼in) sheet of pale coral card

One 30 x 21cm (12 x 8¼in) sheet of gold card

One sheet of country cottage-themed decoupage, including a 10.5 x 14.8cm (4⅛ x 5⅞in) sheet of backing paper

One small white doily

Two sheets of white shrink plastic

Four different afternoon tea stamps

Archival royal blue inkpad

Silicone glue and cocktail stick

Tweezers

Double-sided tape

Bone folder and scoring tool

Guillotine and sharp scissors

Acrylic mounting block

Heat tool

2 Cut out the main picture and the backing paper from the decoupage sheet, and mount both on gold card. Use the guillotine to trim the gold card down until there is only a 5mm (⅛in) border round each.

3 Stick the mounted backing paper piece to the main card with double-sided tape. Attach the paper doily to the bottom right of the centre of the card using silicone glue.

4 Use the sharp scissors to carefully cut out the decoupage pieces. Give them each a slight curve with your finger.

5 Stick the mounted main picture to the main card as shown, then use silicone glue and a cocktail stick to attach the decoupage pieces in turn. The large house is the first layer, and the flowerbed and three pieces of the thatched roof go on top of that.

6 Press the teapot stamp on to the archival inkpad, then press it on to the shrink plastic.

7 Use the various designs to stamp two plates, one jam pot and three teacups on to the shrink plastic. Use small sharp scissors to cut out each piece, being extremely careful and cutting as close as you can to the lines. Remember to cut out the inside of the teapot and teacup handle, too.

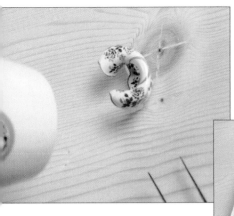

Tip

Never, ever use your heat tool near your craft mat as it will warp it.

Tip

As the plastic shrinks, the colours get darker as the pigments get closer together. Bear this in mind when picking your ink colour, and go for a shade lighter than you would like the finished piece to end up.

8 Hold one of the pieces on a heatproof surface with your tweezers, and use the heat tool to shrink it. It will curl up, but do not lose your nerve! Keep heating it until it flattens back out. Immediately place the large acrylic block on top of it to make sure that it is completely flat (see inset) and turn off your heat tool.

9 Repeat with all of the shrink plastic pieces.

10 Use silicone glue to mount the shrink plastic pieces on to the doily to finish.

Silhouette Builders

This new home card has an unusual twist: fairy folk building a little home.

Rose Cottage

Real pressed roses and leaves twist round this unashamedly romantic new home card with more English cottages!

Roses Round the Door

A lovely bright red die-cut front door has been made into a shaker card with little blossoms behind the acetate.

An Overseas Home

This card was designed for those making a move overseas. The lady is gazing fondly over the water towards her old home.

Christmas Card

Christmas is one of my favourite times of year and this card says it all. The glittery snow sums up a white Christmas beautifully for me!

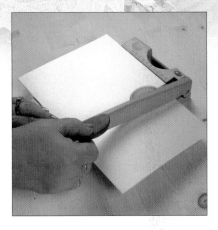

1 Fold the white card in half, sharpen the crease with a bone folder and trim to 18 x 21cm (7 x 8¼in) using a guillotine.

YOU WILL NEED

One 30 x 21cm (12 x 8¼in) church scene picture

One 30 x 21cm (12 x 8¼in) sheet of red pearly card

One 30 x 21cm (12 x 8¼in) sheet of antique gold card

One 42 x 30cm (16½ x 12in) sheet of white pearl card

Snowy glitter

15mm (½in) burgundy ribbon

7mm (¼in) gold ribbon

Small adhesive craft jewels

Glue pen

2mm (1/32in) foam tape

Double-sided tape

Guillotine

Bone folder

Scissors

Glue pen

There are several brands of glue pen, but all are basically just that: glue in a pen. It appears blue but then dries clear. As it is in a pen, it is easy to apply, even to smaller areas of your card – I think this is a must-have tool!

2 Cut out the largest church scene, and make a gold mount for it that is 5mm (¼in) larger all round. Secure the scene to the front of the mount with double-sided tape.

3 Make a red mount for the piece that is 10mm (½in) larger than the gold mount; then make a second gold mount 5mm (¼in) larger than the red mount. Secure the piece to the red mount with 2mm (¹⁄₃₂in) foam tape; then attach it all to the second gold mount using double-sided tape.

4 Place foam tape on the back of the larger gold mount, remove the backing and place on the front of the card.

5 Open up the card and place the two ribbons against the spine, using them as one (see inset). Close the card and tie a bow to hold the ribbon in place. Trim away any excess ribbon using the scissors.

6 Use the glue pen to scribble over the snowy areas on the picture.

7 Sprinkle glitter over the whole piece. Tap off any excess and leave to dry.

From left to right:

The Snow Family

This lovely stamped and coloured card features a snowman couple. The smaller image below is done on shrink plastic (see pages 108–109 for the technique).

Christmas Angel

This angelic little girl is one of my favourite Christmas-themed images. The diagonal cutaway style gives a different twist to a traditional card.

Christmas Cooking!

Another of my favourite vintage Christmas images with an enthusiastic little girl baking Christmas cookies – so sweet!

Happy Anniversary

This light-hearted decoupaged card with its vintage photographs makes a lovely anniversary card and the lace and pearl embellishments add that romantic touch to complete the effect.

1 Keep one of the pictures intact. Cut the lady and gentleman out of the second, and cut out just the upper body of the lady and her parasol from the third.

YOU WILL NEED

Two 30 x 21cm (12 x 8¼in) sheets of duck-egg blue card

One 30 x 21cm (12 x 8¼in) sheet of antique gold card

One 30 x 21cm (12 x 8¼in) sheet of off-white card

Three identical Victorian-style photographs of a courting couple

Paper lace ribbons

Self-adhesive pearls

15mm (½in) bronze ribbon

7mm (¼in) pale blue ribbon

Tweezers

Double-sided tape

Foam tape

Guillotine

Scissors

Bone folder and scoring board

Silicone glue

2 Attach the intact picture to off-white card with double-sided tape, then trim, leaving a 5mm (⅛in) border all round. Repeat the process with duck-egg blue card, again allowing for a 5mm (⅛in) border.

3 Fold the sheet of duck-egg blue card in half and use a bone folder to sharpen the crease.

4 Cut a piece of gold card to 14 x 20cm (5½ x 7⅞in), then peel the backing from the lace ribbon and stick a strip down one of the long sides. Tuck the ends of the ribbon behind the card, then attach a second strip across the bottom, tidily tucking the ends behind as before.

5 Attach the gold card to the folded blue card, using 2mm (⅟₃₂in) foam tape; then attach the mounted picture on top of the gold card, again using 2mm (⅟₃₂in) foam tape.

6 Apply the pearl strips along the lace ribbon. You may need to apply a few single pearls to ensure a neat finish.

7 Tie the bronze and blue ribbons along the spine of the card, making sure that the bow ends up where there is most space in the centre of the photograph. Treat both as a single ribbon to make it easier for yourself.

8 Give the second picture (lady and gentleman) a gentle curve with your fingers and attach it to the card with silicone glue (see inset).

9 Curve and secure the top piece in the same way to finish the card. Remember to allow the card to dry overnight before putting it in an envelope.

This is the centre of the Dancing with Shadows card, which has a pop-out section.

Clockwise from left:

Heartfelt Greetings
The hearts are stamped and embossed with gold embossing powder, then cut out to make this elegant and sophisticated anniversary card.

Gatefold Silhouettes
Identical images have been paired here to make the cover of the card and then a silver-embossed Victorian doily image has been stamped inside the card.

Dancing with Shadows
This card has a lovely centre (see the inset) and the cover is decorated with miniature flowers and a simple topper.

Anniversary Ribbons
This card has a lovely unusual fold that can be used for lots of different themes.

Congratulations

Old family photographs, or vintage photographs that you have collected, can be used very effectively in making cards – here the same young man is pictured as a boy and then an adult, and the photographs are used together as an exam congratulations card.

YOU WILL NEED

Two 30 x 21cm (12 x 8¼in) sheets of gold mirror card

One 21 x 15cm (8¼ x 6in) sheet of William Morris design backing paper

One 42 x 30cm (16½ x 12in) sheet of dark brown card

Suitable photographs

Embellishments (in this case two buttons and a key)

Double-sided sticky tape

Guillotine

Silicone glue and cocktail stick

Bone folder

Foam tape

1 Fold the brown card in half and sharpen the crease with a bone folder. Use a guillotine to cut the card down to 21 x 16.5cm (8¼ x 6½in).

2 Cut a 20 x 15.5cm (7⅞ x 6⅛in) piece of gold card; and a 19 x 14.5cm (7½ x 5¾in) piece of William Morris backing paper. Mount the backing paper on the gold card with double-sided tape.

3 Attach 2mm (¹⁄₃₂in) foam tape to the back of the gold card, then peel off the backing and attach it to the front of the card.

4 Mount the main photograph on gold card, as in step 2, leaving a 5mm (1/8in) border of gold showing, then attach it to the front of the card with double-sided sticky tape.

5 Use the guillotine to crop the smaller photograph so that it fits well in the remaining space (see inset), then mount it on gold card and secure it to the front of the card with double-sided tape.

6 Embellish the card with the key and buttons, securing them with silicone glue.

Da Vinci Card

These drawings by Leonardo da Vinci make an excellent masculine background for an exam congratulations card.

Vintage Seal

A collection of lovely vintage bits and pieces are used here, with a faux wax seal, a stamped book and sepia photo – ideal for an older person's success maybe?

Index